Now I Can SEE The Light

Dr. Marcia T. Caton

ISBN: 978-1-7345107-5-1

Cover Design & Illustrations: Illustrated by Lynda V. McKen-
zie"

This title is available as an E-book. It is also available via online retailers.

Printed in the United States of America.

CONTENTS

Acknowledgments

For my supporters, Marcia T. Caton, Cynthia Gordon, and Claudia Stanley thank you for your time, patience, and love. Each of you plays a unique and immeasurable role in my life. Servant of God Marcia Tenn, Pastors Ean Mayne, and Fitzroy Porter, your spiritual guidance and encouragement have been invaluable.

I want to express my appreciation to Dr. Lorraine Emeghebo for editing the book.

I dedicate this book to my lovely wife, Arnetta, my life support, you have been the rock of my life, and without you, there is no me.

Finally, to God for guiding me, especially those days when it was challenging to remain focused.

Foreword

Clive,

I believe that I have been prepared for the role as your caregiver because of my journey before meeting you. I have watched you persevere through many hardships, adjusting to your new normal and moving around the environment without your sight. You have undergone many treatments and surgeries, and not once have I ever heard you complain. Instead, you use it as an opportunity to strengthen your faith and to become closer to Jesus Christ.

From my first memory of you, I have watched you take baby steps to draw closer to Jesus Christ and then, in 2013, recommit yourself to him. Subsequently, you have worked diligently to learn Jesus' divine words. We have both discovered that the Bible is full of information on daily living, but it can be challenging to interpret. Nonetheless, you spend your waking hours learning the Bible's inspirational words and displaying behaviors reflective of Jesus Christ's characteristics. One of our relationship's beautiful components is that we partner together to become more familiar with the Bible and bring its teachings to others.

The Bible verse, "My brethren, count it all joy when you fall into various trials, knowing that the testing of your faith produces patience. But let patience have *its* perfect work, that you may be perfect and complete, lacking nothing" (James 1:2–4 NKJV), which helps me to depend more on Jesus Christ and face our challenges with confidence that Christ the Provider will never abandon us. Although life has dealt you a pill that some individuals would have had difficulty swallowing, you have remained positive, not allowing circumstances to dictate your personality. Most importantly, you have never taken on the victimization syndrome. I am frequently amused when I hear you motivate others to persevere through their trials and tribulations. In my perspective, you are a role model, hero, and survivor.

What an incredible and inspiring journey you have walked, and I am happy that you have an opportunity to share it with the world. I hope your journey will inspire others and that you continue to grow closer to Jesus Christ.

Your loving wife, Arnetta

Preface

I came to the United States from Jamaica, West Indies, at the beginning of the millennium to participate in a family member's wedding. I was excited to have the opportunity to visit because coming to this country had been a long-term goal. My visit was filled with excitement and adventure. I toured many historical sites that I had studied in high school history classes, and it was a fantastic experience—transferring my knowledge of the places to reality.

When I returned home, the idea of immigrating to the US resurfaced in my thoughts because I yearned to be with my family members. Subsequently, I spoke to my family members about moving there, and of course, they were ecstatic about the idea. However, one of the "older heads" in the family suggested that I should have a goal for moving to keep my focus. I had always wanted a college education, and the US was the perfect country to pursue my dream because of its citizens' educational opportunities. Consequently, I spent a lot of time researching possible career positions and linked those job titles to specific US colleges.

After putting everything in place to leave Jamaica in 2001, I went on my way to the US to pursue my lifelong dream of becoming a mechanical engineer. I wanted to hit the ground running, so I spent the first week exploring and learning my new environment: Queens, New York. Since one of my goals was to go to college, I wanted to start working immediately to save money for expenses.

The following week, I started job hunting, which was challenging because I didn't have an employment history in the US. However, after approaching the local restaurant owner several times for a job, I was finally allowed to prove myself. My primary responsibility was doing odd jobs and assisting the cook. While doing so, I discovered that I enjoyed cooking, and I wanted to become better at it. I took advantage of every opportunity to work with the cook, even when it was off the clock and without financial compensation.

Shortly afterward, the cook got a better offer at another restaurant and quit. I was promoted to cook and worked twelve hours a day, seven days a week, preparing dishes for approximately 250 people daily during the week, and many more on the weekends. I loved my job and was fortunate to be working with a great group of people.

Little did I know that this job in a new country would be the start of a long journey in pursuit of a life that honors and obeys Jesus Christ. This book, *Now I Can SEE the Light*, will reflect on my process of growth in living specific Christian qualities found in the Book of Galatians. I also want to share how these traits have helped me in my relationships with others and in putting things in perspective.

As I continue to mature, I hope to become more of an advocate, peacemaker, healer, and restorer in a world that can be challenging to navigate. May Jesus Christ bless you as you walk with me on this journey.

Clive

Chapter 1

Once I was settled in the United States and was promoted to cook, my skills improved rapidly, and over time I gained my employer's confidence. I planned to continue working at the restaurant while attending college. However, in 2002, I began to experience occasional episodes of double vision with severe headaches. I ignored the symptoms because I thought they were temporary, and I did not have health insurance.

When the headaches became more severe, I took over-the-counter painkillers, and the ache subsided. However, the episodes of diminished vision became more frequent. One particular day, I had my first frightening experience: I heard and could recognize my coworker's voice, but for a short time, I could not see her.

While walking home later that day, I temporarily lost my vision again. When it returned, I was horrified to find myself in the middle of a bustling street. I became fearful about what was going to happen next. At the urging of family members and their support, I visited a neurologist (a doctor specializing in the brain). The doctor ordered an MRI (Magnetic Resonance Imaging)—an x-ray of the brain. It revealed that a tumor was pressing on the area controlling my vision.

Medical Issues Begin

Learning about the tumor was unsettling. Nevertheless, the doctor assured me that the tumor could be removed without complication because of advances in technology, and the recovery period would be uneventful. Within three weeks, my first of many surgeries was performed to remove the growth, and I spent one week in the hospital afterward. My post-operative period was uneventful, as promised, and the headaches and vision problems were gone. Once again, my eyesight was crystal clear. I returned to my day-to-day activities, which included working at the restaurant.

However, in 2003, I began experiencing the same symptoms of vision loss and headaches. Initially, I thought it was a dream, and I tried to ignore it. *This loss of vision has to be temporary!* But after several repeat occurrences of the same symptoms, I returned to my neurologist. He stated that the tumor's return was not uncommon in a small percentage of patients. He further assured me that whatever was going on in my brain could be successfully addressed. The doctor ordered another MRI, which revealed that the tumor had not only returned but had grown more aggressively and was more extensive than before. My confidence about having a positive outcome from a second surgery was a bit shattered, but I remained hopeful that the next time around would be different.

Thus, in 2004 the doctor performed a second surgery. Unfortunately, the recovery phase was much more eventful than that of the first surgery. I was readmitted to the hospital three times due to unexpected complications. Furthermore, I experienced heavy bleeding from the area of my body where the skin had been removed to graft onto the incision site on my head. I was also unable to climb stairs. This post-surgical period was a tough time for me. Slowly the complications subsided, and I once again returned to work. Sadly, the outcome was also different from the previous one: my vision was unclear, though I could read and see objects.

I continued working at the restaurant, but in 2008, my vision deteriorated once again. Another MRI revealed that the tumor had returned for the third time, so a third surgery was scheduled in 2009. After this surgery, my vision returned with even less clarity than before. The possibility of losing my sight became real, and along with that, my anxiety levels also increased.

At this time, a new team of doctors offered a different approach to treating the tumor growth: surgical intervention followed by rounds of radiation. Even though I had renewed hope for this surgery's successful outcome, I hesitated to make an immediate decision. But what choice did I have? If I did nothing, I would surely lose my sight, so I had the fourth surgery in 2011. The doctors found that the tumor had become more embedded in the area of my brain responsible for vision, and they were unable to remove the entire growth. The extensive surgery needed would have tremendously reduced my chances of regaining my sight. Nonetheless, I had the surgery and after the procedure, I took the radiation therapy and continued taking it for a while, hoping that it might eventually shrink the tumor. That did not happen. In 2015, some family members encouraged me to visit a neurologist in another region of the country to evaluate my case. Although I was hesitant, I once again saw a group of physicians who reviewed my medical records. They discovered that the tumor had shrunk approximately 50 percent since the last surgery and suggested that I undergo a fifth surgery.

After much deliberation, I declined. Reflecting on previous operations and the protracted post-op periods—especially after the second surgery—discouraged me from accepting another surgical attempt. Nonetheless, in 2016, the same doctors suggested that I join a clinical trial of new medications to reduce the tumor's size. Although I had some trepidation about participating because of the drugs' side effects, I accepted and took the prescribed medications.

No More Surgery

Fast forward to now, I completed taking the experimental drugs, and the size of the tumor remained the same. I am legally blind, which is otherwise known as having low vision. I can see shadows and recognize others by their voice. However, my biggest challenge has been my visual perception. Because I can see a little bit, initially, I believed that I could see more than I really could. Fighting against the vision loss caused me to bump into, trip over, or knock over things.

Although my vision has wavered between "okay" and "poor" for the last decade, I had the pleasure of being able to see before my vision loss. While that was a privilege, the transition from the sighted world to the low-vision world has been difficult. I wake up each day, having to navigate within my home and the outside world. These actions used to be second nature to me. My primary goal is to be able to move around safely and not hurt myself. Something as necessary as cleaning my teeth is a struggle if my toothbrush location has been changed.

On one of my down days, a keynote speaker at a mayoral event—for employers who hire disabled individuals—changed my viewpoint about my situation. The speaker, who was disabled and had earned a Ph.D., said, "Do not accept the handicap label. Aspire to rise above the label." Her words comforted me. I did not want to spend my time having a pity party because my low vision was out of my control. I gained hope that my experiences could be an inspiration for others who have had significant life changes.

Turning My Attention to Jesus Christ

On the positive note I had a lot of downtime to contemplate my life. One issue I pinpointed was that I needed a closer relationship with Jesus Christ. My Christian journey during my early years had been bumpy, with highs and lows. When I was a child, my parents belonged to the Baptist church, and naturally, I became a member of that community. We attended services weekly, observed the rituals, and participated in various church activities. However, I never got baptized.

Then a strange thing happened in the 1990s. A prediction said that the world was coming to an end, and I grew fearful that I would not be ready to meet Jesus. This fear strongly influenced my decision to become baptized, and so in 1999, I professed Christ as my savior and was baptized into the Baptist Protestant denomination. One Baptist tenet is that the Bible is the only authority. The significance of the Bible is in 2 Timothy 3:16–17: "All Scripture is God-breathed and is useful for teaching, rebuking, correcting and training in righteousness, so that the servant of God may be thoroughly equipped for every good work" (NIV).

One of my first tasks was to become acquainted with Jesus Christ's nature, as described in the Bible, and to integrate more of his characteristics in my life. Unfortunately, my life subsequently diverged into several different paths, which is not unusual during life. All my determined plans to reshape my Christian journey fell by the wayside and became less of a priority.

After my second surgery in 2004, the presence of Jesus' words began to surface with intensity in my life. This post-surgical period was so difficult that my need to hold on to something bigger than life became inextricably linked to my survival. I reached out to my pastor in New York and told him that I was ready to recommit myself to Jesus, and subsequently did in 2013. Jesus Christ, my savior, continues to be ever-present in my life, and since then, I have been committed to living a life more reflective of Bible teachings.

Sharing My Experiences in Faith

I have also developed a renewed commitment to spreading the words of the Bible to others. My thirst for those words has allowed me to become more focused on the essential things of life. Getting to know Jesus Christ and partaking of his blessings, such as his provisions for my basic needs, enriches my life and the lives of others.

Since my highest priority is to have a more intimate relationship with Jesus, I believe that the only way to develop such a relationship is for my character to better reflect Christ's teachings found in the Bible. Therefore, I have sought to grow and strengthen the spirit that values "love, joy, peace, patience, kindness, goodness, faithfulness, gentleness, self-control …" (Galatians 5:22-23 ESV). To that list, I add forgiveness, wisdom, and gratitude.

These traits can only be a work in progress for any of us. No matter how hard we try to reflect them, perfection is unattainable. But it is the struggle that is important.

My trip through life and the forks in the road I have maneuvered through have been exciting. Furthermore, my renewed spirit has sustained me along the way during my unpredictable journey. While on this journey, the maturing of self-control, love, joy, peace, patience, kindness, goodness, faithfulness, gentleness, forgiveness, wisdom, and gratitude traits have become more important to me to become the best version of my spiritual self. As I continue to mature, I hope to become more of an advocate, peacemaker, healer, and restorer in a world that can be challenging to navigate.

Chapter 2: A Spirit That Values Self-Control

I use the terms *self-control* and *self-discipline* interchangeably. Whenever I think of self-control, what comes to mind is "the ability to muster the inner strength to negate impulses that could lead to behaviors contrary to Bible teachings." The Greek word for *self-control* is *egkrateia*, meaning "having a significant force within but able to control it." The Greek definition reflects many individuals' desire to manage the behavior that might harm themselves and others.

In the New Testament (Galatians 5:22–25), the Apostle Paul identified self-control last in listing the fruit of the Spirit. However, I believe it should be first because of its influence on the maturing of other Christian traits. The other fruit—love, joy, peace, patience, kindness, goodness, faithfulness, and gentleness—cannot be expressed (or learned) without employing self-control. For that matter, neither can forgiveness, wisdom, or gratitude be shown without first mastering self-control as much as humans can. The development and strengthening of the Spirit of self-control continue to be an ongoing process for me. Whenever I can display self-discipline, it motivates me to become better at it.

Control Emphasized

My desire to control my actions started during my formative years. At an early age, I learned that control is an expectation, and failure was not an option. Many other family members and school personnel associated self-control with staying focused, achieving goals, and managing emotions, especially during conflicts. However, remaining focused and achieving goals as a youth were the highest priority for most parents/caretakers.

While in Jamaica, because of sparse resources, gaining entrance into high school was competitive and based on merit, as mandatory secondary education did not exist. Each student who wanted to attend high school had to take a competitive entrance exam. Every parent/caretaker had the goal of positioning their children to pass that entrance exam.

To prepare for this exam, I studied a minimum of three hours every day from Monday to Friday and more hours on the weekend. However, while trying to succeed in school, I encountered many distractions. Other students were also prone to losing focus and interest in what they were trying to study. Even during primary school, noises and actions that distracted me were common, and I struggled to put them in their place. As I matured, I found ways to deal with those disturbances. One of my strategies was to sit alone with my eyes closed for approximately fifteen minutes and repeat this statement: "I will remain focused."

As I approached my teenage years, and the number of my friends increased, remaining focused again became a challenge. My previous strategy of meditating for fifteen minutes wasn't doing the job anymore. I tried placing bold signs with this statement, "Clive will remain focused," in different areas of my room. These "in my face" signs helped me to remain dedicated to my goal—succeeding on the secondary school entrance exam—and I did pass. My success reinforced the idea that there are benefits to being disciplined.

The "rubber hit the road" concerning self-control when I recommitted myself to serving Jesus Christ. The only way to become connected to Jesus is by reading the Bible. However, when I started to delve deeper, I became overwhelmed with the amount of information and the challenge of interpreting it. Because of my high school journey, I knew that if I remained disciplined, I would succeed. No task would be impossible. As I meditated on the importance of staying disciplined to get to know Jesus Christ, the story of Bartimaeus in Mark 10:46–52 came to my mind. Bartimaeus, a blind man, understood Jesus' characteristics and trusted him. That trust led to the healing of his blindness, and then he became a disciple. I decided that like Bartimaeus, getting to know Jesus was essential because I desire to follow him.

Devotion to Jesus Christ

Another area that I work on is making sure Jesus Christ is my priority each day. So I am careful to start my day with prayers. I find that if I postpone my devotion time to later on during the day, there is a chance it will never happen, or I am unable to be focused, and my devotion will be lackluster.

The biblical story that helps me make Jesus my priority each day is in Luke 10—a story about Jesus visiting Martha, Mary, and Lazarus. Most crucial is verse 42—"Mary has chosen the good part, which will not be taken away from her" (NHEB)—which emphasized the importance of placing my devotion above all other actions and responsibilities.

Although I had heard that prayer would change my relationship with Jesus Christ, the change became evident when I started to spend more leisurely time with him. Soon it became natural for me to kneel and unload my challenges to him as needed throughout the day. I gained many benefits from this unique relationship. When I became overwhelmed, I could pray anytime and anywhere. After my dedicated time with Jesus Christ, I felt less stressed.

During this part of my Christian journey, I quickly discovered that recommitting myself to Jesus Christ was an easy task. The hard part was following up with action. To remain steadfast with my promise, I recommit myself to Jesus Christ each day through devotion. Do I get up each day with a high energy level to praise God? Not every day. Whenever human nature takes over, I say a short prayer, but I make sure I remain committed to my daily ritual.

In addition to spending more time with Jesus, I also developed the habit of responding to anxiety with prayer. In the past, I became anxious when a family member was not available to transport me to church, to a Bible study, or other necessary destinations. But with practice, I was able to replace anxiety with Christ's words. One of my favorite verses is Psalm 46:1, which says, "God is our refuge and strength, a very present help in trouble" (ESV). In studying the Bible routinely, I have developed a keener sense of hearing the words, which allows me to memorize them. Also with the advancement of technology, I can listen to the words of the Bible 24/7 on my smartphone.

My Spiritual Family

One of my goals was to develop a passion for Jesus Christ because I recognized that this type of excitement had paved the way for my daily devotion. My love for Jesus extended to my church community, and my spiritual family members became an integral part of my inner circle. I worked hard to make sure that my facial expression reflects the love for Jesus so that others would be inspired to know him. I can say with confidence that I have become disciplined regarding the works of Jesus Christ.

On the lighter side, I have heard several pastors repeat this statement: "Jesus Christ has a sense of humor. Whenever you are confident that you have perfected a challenging skill, you will be put to the test." Guess what! My test involved the church community.

I had a smooth and uneventful transition into my church community. However, I quickly learned that it could be a fertile soil that breeds contention among members. One of the root causes is the rumor mill. I should not have been surprised because the Bible warns us in several verses that the tongue is the most uncontrollable body area. It can easily cause irreparable damage. One example of such Bible verses is in James 3:8: "But no man can tame the tongue. It is an unruly evil, full of deadly poison" (NKJV).

Nevertheless, finding this out in person disturbed me because I believed that the church environment should be the most peaceful place on earth. Jesus Christ is love, and every Christian aspires to develop and imitate his traits. However, I quickly learned that this "unruly evil" results from people with different perspectives, needs, and wants. This mixture can prevent the union of a church community that should exist. I also discovered that one of the causes for the division in my church was the misunderstandings of individuals' intentions.

Some church leaders openly discuss the vulnerability of church communities as it relates to becoming embroiled in conflicts. One pattern of disputes that I recognized in my church is that the involved parties try to rally other congregants' support, pitting one against the other. If this hemorrhaging does not stop, the division among spiritual family members widens.

Whenever a member of my congregation complains about another member, I have become more disciplined in listening and not taking sides. Being much more attuned to the devil's plan, the architect of division, instead I encourage unity and oneness in the community.

Christian Unity

The survival of a church community is contingent on the members getting along with each other. The Apostle Paul sent warnings to the early century Christians about potential divisions and the importance of unity in the church. One of the verses highlighting this message is in Galatians 3:28: “There is neither Jew nor Greek, there is neither slave nor free, there is neither male nor female; for you are all one in Christ Jesus” (NKJV).

I have become much better at deflating conflicts among my spiritual family members. I diligently try to put out any fires before the disagreement penetrates the community. I respond with Bible verses and, if the opportunity presents itself, offer alternative viewpoints. I have had many successes in this area and the occasional failure.

As the Bible's teachings have become integrated into my life, one of my goals is to continue to exercise self-control. Whenever my behavior falls short, first, I apologize to Jesus and ask for help in that area. I also apologize to myself. I need to understand that I do not have control over others' behavior, nor over the individual(s) involved in a disagreement, even if they have promised to try harder, not to take offense so easily.

Prayer

Jesus Christ, I want you to increase my self-control. Whenever I am lacking in that area, help me to become aware and work harder at it. Allow me to display self-control when temptation arises. In the name of Jesus Christ, we pray, amen!

Chapter 3: A Spirit That Values Love

The concept of love dated back to ancient civilizations and was developed by nurturing one's offspring and caring for the family. However, over the years, advertisements and mass media have commercialized love. Nowadays, it is so easy to confuse feelings of love with infatuation or lust.

The Greeks identified four types of love:

- *Eros*—romantic love
- *Philia*—friendship love
- *Storge*—family affection
- *Agape*—selfless love

According to ancient Greeks, the highest form of love is agape; it is selfless, sacrificial, and unconditional love. Agape is the type of love that Jesus Christ wants Christians to possess, so it is encouraged by most religious/spiritual traditions. Unfortunately, self-centeredness has become pervasive today, and thus, the display of agape love seems almost impossible for many individuals.

There are several definitions of "love" in contemporary society, and the word means different things to different people. Furthermore, the term love can be used as a verb (actions) or a noun (feelings). In some ways, it is held up as the magical balm for everything in life, yet the basics of love—nurturing one's offspring and caring for the family—have fallen by the wayside.

Some human beings are preoccupied with feelings of love. Consequently, the behavior is magnified in the types of songs that have been pervasive on the *Billboard* charts for decades. Some of the popular love song titles from the 1960s through the 1980s were:

- Can't Take My Eyes Off of You"
- "Ain't No Mountain High Enough"
- "When a Man Loves a Woman"
- "Endless Love"
- "Keep On Loving You"

During the 2000s, love songs continue to climb the *Billboard* charts with titles such as:

- "Crazy In Love With You"
- "We Belong Together"
- "You Are Beauty"

Why is there such a focus on love? Because the famous adage tells us that we have nothing and are nothing without love. Even the Bible tells us we can have many things, but if we "have not love, I am nothing" (1 Corinthians 13:2 ESV).

Worldly Love vs. Christian Love

In my opinion, the Christian life can be summarized in three words: "GOD IS LOVE" (1 John 4:8 ESV). God's Love is mystical. It is not a light-headed feeling, but our life should nevertheless be transformed by it. The Bible has a blueprint for Love, and the word is referenced approximately 750 times from Genesis to Revelation. However, this type of Love is not based on action—the verb form of the term. And more importantly, it does not fluctuate. Jesus Christ commands his children to love one another in Matthew 22:39: "Thou shalt love thy neighbor as thyself" (ASV). In other words, we should treat other people the way we want to be treated. Jesus also directs us to love our enemies in Matthew 5:44: "But I say unto you, love your enemies, bless them that curse you, do good to them that hate you, and pray for them which despitefully use you, and persecute you" (KJV).

Loving our neighbor is not an option; we are to love even the most challenging person under all circumstances. The type of Love Jesus Christ has for his children can be found in John 15:13—"Greater love hath no man than this, that a man lay down his life for his friends" (KJV)…. and John 3:16, "For God so loved the world, that he gave his only begotten Son, that whosoever believeth in him should not perish, but have everlasting life" (KJV).

On the cross, Jesus' death is the most significant display of Love, that one person can show for people. We are to use Jesus Christ's Love for us, his children, as a model to love others. The Apostle Paul provides a perfect example of Love in 1 Corinthians 13:4–7: "Love is patient, Love is kind. It does not envy; it does not boast; it is not proud. It does not dishonor others; it is not self-seeking, it is not easily angered, it keeps no record of wrongs. Love does not delight in evil but rejoices with the truth. It always protects, always trusts, always hopes, always perseveres" (NIV).

"Love Thy Neighbor"

Although I strive to love others, I admit that I frequently avoid problematic people. Is that displaying love for them? There is obvious room for improvement in this area for me. I occasionally ponder: How can I develop a love that is enduring and undiminished? Relationships can be challenging to start but easy to evaporate. How can I use the Bible as a model to improve my ability to give unconditional love, especially to those who seem unlovable?

Because I wanted to increase my ability to love others unconditionally, my spiritual journey begins assessing my relationship with Jesus Christ. My love for Jesus Christ dramatically influences the relationships I have with others. I also need to pay ongoing attention to my relationship with Jesus, so it does not diminish unnoticed.

I meditate on the following questions:

❖ How has learning more about the Bible definition of love transformed my life?

❖ How does my trust in Jesus drive out the fear of being with difficult individuals?

❖ In what ways am I spreading the kind of love defined by Jesus Christ?

Second, I contemplate my relationship with myself, particularly self-care. These questions assist with this evaluation:

- ❖ Do I set aside me time for myself … doing nothing, just relaxing?
- ❖ Do I eat quality, nutritious foods?
- ❖ Do I spend time with family and friends?
- ❖ Do I exercise?
- ❖ Do I have someone to talk to if I'm feeling overwhelmed?
- ❖ Do I make time to do fun things?

Lastly, I contemplate my relationship with my spouse. In this part of my life, these questions are helpful:

- ❖ Are we partners and friends?
- ❖ Do we have difficulty communicating?
- ❖ Do we spend quality time together?
- ❖ Do we manage conflict in healthy ways?
- ❖ Do we share household chores?
- ❖ Do we consistently pray together?
- ❖ Do we study the Bible together?
- ❖ Do we set aside date time?

- ❖ Do we show appreciation for each other?
- ❖ Do we agree to disagree in respectful ways?
- ❖ Are we tolerant of each other's shortcomings?

I firmly believe that no one can love others unconditionally until their relationships with Jesus Christ, themselves, and their spouse reflect Bible teachings. If those relationships are on shaky ground, a person will not nurture and support others. There is always room for improvement, so with Christ's grace, I will eventually be better able to love all people unconditionally, as the Bible teaches.

Prayer

Jesus Christ, one of my biggest challenges in life is to love those who seem unlovable. I want to be obedient to your command that says to "love your neighbor as yourself." As you work miracles in my broken heart, help me to love others as the Bible teaches us.

In Jesus' name, amen!

Chapter 4: A Spirit That Values Joy

The Greek word for *joy* is *chara*, meaning "gladness multiplied greatly." The standard definition of joy in modern society is "experiencing a good feeling." Many times individuals confuse the emotions of joy and happiness, leading to the words being used interchangeably. Some individuals may speak of experiencing happiness in a relationship, attending a concert, and achieving goals. However, this type of joy is from outside of ourselves. It is also temporal because the emotion is dependent on circumstances, according to the Apostle Paul.

However, in the Christian community, the term "joy" tends to be used more frequently because biblical figures, like Apostle Paul, encourage believers to seek joy. The Bible explains that happiness is dependent on outward circumstances, while what is going on outside of individuals does not influence their joy.

Finding My Joy

The pursuit of inner joy, even under challenging conditions, became an important area of growth for me during my spiritual journey. Other believers often pursue this quality as well because of its long-lasting effects. I discovered that when I allowed outward circumstances to influence my joy, my life was emotionally "topsy-turvy."

It is not uncommon for others to ask me how I can have joy with my low vision. This kind of negative question can affect my joy if I let it, so I have become determined not to allow this question and my circumstances to influence my joy. I try hard not to focus on my trials and tribulations and instead try to see the new possibilities this predicament might offer. I want to show others, especially non-believers, that my life has not been placed on hold because of my blindness, and that I can find joy along the way. I hope that when others see the happiness radiating from me, they might also want to experience inward joy in their lives.

One of my approaches to increasing my joy has been to become more familiar with Apostle Paul's Christian walk. His epistle to the Philippians became central to my understanding of what it takes to have joy under any circumstances. Paul, the apostle, wrote the four chapters of this letter to the first congregation founded in Europe. Although Paul was under house arrest in Rome and might have been facing martyrdom, the words "joy" and "rejoice" appear many times. Paul's fate was in the hands of those who imprisoned him, but it is clear that his circumstances did not influence his authentic feeling of joy. Paul also emphasized to Christians that life's journey has many forks in the road. We can either let those forks determine our feelings, or use them to rejoice in Jesus Christ.

Another helpful action was to reflect on the patterns of joy in my life. During these periods of meditation, it became easier to identify the happy and dispirited times in my life. People on the outside might have seen me as joyful when I was successful with my high school entrance exam, got a prestigious job following high school, and fulfilled the requirements for immigrating to the U.S, but that is because they were confusing happiness with joy. I was not experiencing joy—no matter how happy or excited I felt—because external circumstances dictated the emotion. I became determined to change this narrative in my life and not allow situations to rob me of inward joy. Because of this decision, I felt empowered.

Joy in the Bible

The Bible became the weapon for bringing enduring joy into my life. Many verses speak about joy. It is not surprising that there are approximately 500 references to joy in the Bible, and Jesus promises us that joy is a byproduct of having a personal relationship with him. During my daily devotions, I pray for healing, opportunities to serve Jesus, and restorations in areas of my life that have been broken.

When dealing with the challenges of blindness, I never ask, "Why me?" Instead, I surrender this stumbling block to Jesus Christ and ask him for a cheerful heart during all circumstances. Some of the comforting Bible verses that have reached deep into my heart are:

- ❖ Deuteronomy 31:6—"Be strong and courageous. Do not be afraid or terrified because of them, for the LORD goes with you; he will never leave you nor forsake you" (NIV).

- ❖ Proverbs 17:22—"A merry heart does good, *like* medicine, but a broken spirit dries the bones" (NKJV).

- ❖ Jeremiah 29:11—"For I know the plans I have for you," declares the LORD, "plans to prosper you and

> not to harm you, plans to give you hope and a future" (NIV).

Another heartfelt Bible verse is James 1:2. "Consider it pure joy, my brothers and sisters, whenever you face trials of many kinds" (NIV).

These verses help me look at my blindness through a spiritual lens, and when I ponder on them through that perspective, I become more confident that Jesus Christ will use my lack of sight to serve his purpose. Learning about other blind individuals such as Helen Keller, Stevie Wonder, and Andrea Bocelli, who have changed the world, strengthened my self-assurance.

Joy and Jesus Christ

The fundamental basis for joy in my life has been to do the will of Jesus Christ. I openly talk about my relationship with Jesus and experience joy when I bring others to him. Furthermore, I primarily speak about him as a joyful person, such as when he used ordinary people to advance the gospel, like in the Parable of the Lost Sheep. This parable appears in the Gospels of Matthew (Matthew 18:12–14) and Luke (Luke 15:3–7). It is the story of a shepherd leaves his flock of ninety-nine sheep to find the lost one. And when the shepherd finds the sheep, he joyfully puts it on his shoulders and goes home. This story is one example of Jesus' joy in response to believers returning to him, found in Luke 15:6—"Rejoice with me; I have found my lost sheep" (NIV). When my actions or display of feelings assist new members in joining the church or encouraging those who have been absent to come back, I rejoice along with Jesus Christ.

My focus now is on being a bearer of joy for others. My progress in this biblical quality has advanced because people say that I exude joy, and some have asked for my "recipe"! I consistently respond to this query by encouraging them to become familiar with the Apostle Paul's Christian journey and discover how they can integrate the methods Paul used to cope with the curveballs in his life to develop and increase his joy.

Notably, Paul did not allow life's challenges to determine his attitude or actions. The more of us who can display his behavior, the better the world will be. Interestingly, Pierre Teilhard De Chardin, a Jesuit priest and philosopher, once said that "Joy is the infallible sign of the presence of God."[2] Each day I try to allow joy to radiate from me.

Prayer

Jesus Christ, help me to find joy when it appears to be far away. Help me to become a beacon of joy in the lives of others. Fill me with everlasting joy and allow sadness, the feeling of rejection, and regrets to flee from me. In Jesus' name, amen!

Chapter 5: A Spirit That Values Inner Peace

The term "peace" has been associated with people living in harmony with each other. Merriam-Webster's Collegiate Dictionary defines peace as "a state of tranquility or quiet," and the Greek word for *peace*, *eiréné*, translates to "quietness and rest."

Some individuals have the idea that peace is elusive because although twentieth-century heads of countries—more than leaders in any other era—have sought peace, the world remains chaotic. Civil wars, ethnic cleansing, racial strife, family conflict, and workplace violence are evident all over the world. Is peace really that elusive? Albert Einstein said, "Peace cannot be kept by force; it can only be achieved by understanding."[3] His words serve as a reminder that a lot of work needs to be done to increase understanding between each other.

Benefits of Peace

I love the song "Let There Be Peace on Earth," and the lyrics continue "… and let it begin with me."[4] The words speak to my basic need for peace. So many benefits are available to an individual when they take the time for a worthwhile quest for inner peace. The calm and serenity they experience will positively affect every system of the body, but the brain benefits the most. Inner peace can rewire the brain, letting it learn to remain calm during the chaos, which makes body systems less vulnerable to disease.[5] Although it may be difficult to find peace because the world appears to be spinning out of control, it is possible … because peace begins with you and me.

I learned a lesson regarding the importance of peace from the late Steven McDonald. McDonald was a New York City Police Department patrolman who was shot and paralyzed by a fifteen-year-old boy on July 12, 1986.[6] Although one might argue that this story is about forgiveness, in my opinion, it is also about how to create a peaceful mindset. After the incident, Steven publicly forgave the young man who shot him and corresponded with him in prison. Later on, in their relationship, the young man apologized to Steven and his wife for his action.

Steven spoke about forgiveness to many audiences across the globe, and at one of the venues, he said that if he had not forgiven the person who shot him, he would have allowed that person to rob him of his peace. Likewise, I need the virtue of inner peace to deal with my disability. I have never seen Steven—no pun intended—but many of my relatives have met him and his family, and have been inspired by his actions.

Jesus Christ's Words

Since Jesus Christ's gospel is my frame of reference, whenever I think of peace, I reflect on Isaiah 26:3: "You will keep *him* in perfect peace, *Whose* mind *is* stayed *on You* ..." (NKJV). When my mind is focused on Jesus Christ, I feel at peace. But since anxious thoughts rob me of that inner peace, I had to find ways to decrease my anxiety. As I said earlier, prayer has helped immensely, but other Bible traits are also very useful.

Besides considering Isaiah 26:3, I have identified four qualities that help me to decrease anxious thoughts so that I can focus on Jesus:

- Self-awareness
- Self-acceptance
- Insight
- Content

Self-awareness assists me in discovering a better understanding of myself. I am better able to avoid triggers that can rob me of my inner peace.

For example, a new environment makes me anxious. Consequently, it is necessary that I become more familiar with a setting before entering.

Self-acceptance gives me the confidence to accept my positive and negative aspects. It is always easy to accept one's positive attributes, but most people are in denial about their negative ones. When we can accept the negative aspects of our personality, we are on the way to finding peace within ourselves.

The relationship of self-awareness, together with **insight,** also affects my decisions. I used to make decisions impulsively, and in retrospect, they were usually more about people-pleasing than what was best for me. Now, no decisions are made without praying for guidance from Jesus. If I experience calmness about my choices, then I believe it is what Jesus Christ wants for me.

Moreover, whenever I experience difficult situations, I refocus and look for the good in the circumstances. In other words, I stop my wandering thoughts of negativity and force myself to find reasons to be grateful. Shifting my thoughts to consider things I can be thankful for—especially when I do not particularly want to find anything to be thankful for—helps increase my inner peace.

Besides, we live in a world where, for many, abundance is the norm. Self-awareness, self-acceptance, and insight have led me to learn how to be **content** with my resources, whether they are small or large.

What Can I Learn?

If a difficulty results from a negative encounter, I ask myself, "What does Jesus Christ want me to learn from this situation?" I listen to televangelists daily, such as Dr. Charles Stanley and Pastors John Gray III and Joseph Prince, and one time I discovered that a discussion on the sermon in Matthew 7:5 was applicable to the growth of my peace.

I do not recall which pastor I was listening to at the time, but he declared that inner peace is our reward when we remove the beam from our eye. Specifically, Matthew 7:5 says, "Thou hypocrite, first cast out the beam out of thine own eye; and then shalt thou see clearly to cast out the mote out of thy brother's eye" (KJV). After an extended discussion on this verse, the pastor implored viewers not to focus on the imperfections of others. Doing so—especially while paying no attention to our own imperfections—will rob us of inner peace.

There are a lot of circumstances and situations that can rob me of inner peace when I am traveling outside my home with the assistance of a white cane. But my level of tension drops whenever I reflect on Jesus Christ, the Prince of Peace. Furthermore, the Bible offers me a blueprint to strengthen my peace. My assurance of his promise of peace is in Proverbs 3:1–2: “My son, forget not my law; but let thine heart keep my commandments: For length of days, and long life, and peace, shall they add to thee” (KJV). And Psalm 119:165: “Great peace have they which love thy law: and nothing shall offend them” (KJV). In the latter, the psalmist assures us that loving and obeying God’s law is a weapon against disharmony. Although the Bible was written many centuries ago, it is still relevant to modern-day living and is the only solution for peace.

Prayer

Jesus Christ, I am in awe of your majesty and creation. Teach me to trust you so that when the storms of life come, I will respond, “All is well.” Continue to slow me down, and no matter what the trials are, help me remember that you are more significant and powerful than they are. In Jesus’ name, amen!

Chapter 6: A Spirit That Values Patience

A lot can be learned about patience from the story of the Chinese bamboo tree. According to legend, the tree did not experience any growth during the first four years, but continued to receive care, nurturing, and love. However, during the fifth year, the tree grew rapidly.

Some commonly asked questions about this tale have been:

- Did the tree experience rapid growth during the fifth year, or did its growth only become apparent to others in that year?

- Was the potential for increase not evident during the first four years simply because it was busy establishing deep roots?

Let us look at the growth of patience. Is the growth of the bamboo tree accurate in reflecting the growth and development of patience? Patience is a virtue that takes commitment and time to blossom fully. Although many individuals experience periodic setbacks when trying to develop this virtue, the search for patience can be beneficial to all.

Slow to Anger

I associate the word "patience" with "slow to anger" and "perseverance." The Greek word for *patience* is *makrothumia*, and some of the translations of this are "forbearance," "long-suffering," and "long-enduring," which agree with my viewpoint. Patience is the key to emotional freedom because when we are patient, we are no longer reacting to others' actions or inaction. Furthermore, with perseverance, we are better able to accept the twists and turns in life, such as traffic jams, non-working elevators, or long lines. Anger and frustration will be thwarted by an individual's mastery of patience. Conversely, being impatient leads to the body, releasing stress hormones that can cause high blood pressure and heart conditions.

I would describe myself as a calm person who does not allow the small stuff of life to ruffle me. If I were asked about my level of patience, I might laud myself for being patient. However, if the truth is known, whenever my patience has been put to the test, it becomes apparent that my mastery of it needs fine-tuning. I am honored to need help with patience because that puts me in the company of a significant Bible figure: Moses.

Even after Moses spent forty years in the desert learning patience and humbleness, he still became impatient with the Israelites when they complained about the water being bitter in Exodus 15:22-26. Furthermore, in Numbers 20:7–13, Moses struck the rock twice in his impatience. Consequently, God became angry with Moses when he struck the rock rather than to follow his instructions of "tell the rock . . . to yield its water." He was too impatient to allow God to show His holiness.

Each new day brings new challenges, and therefore there are lots of chances for me—and everyone! —to become impatient. Being unable to use my phone and missing devotion with my spiritual brothers and sisters are two situations that always test my patience. Being unable to properly use previously learned skills to navigate around in my environment can be maddening. Listening to folks who are blessed complaining about the small stuff of life, and perhaps about a goal of theirs that is not materializing fast enough, eats away at whatever patience I have left.

Bible-Trained Patience

Gaining deeper knowledge about the Bible's teachings has allowed me to gain additional patience. This quality has become vital for me to get through the major and minor irritations in my life. Since I developed the mindset that I will not allow circumstances to control my reactions, I have become more tolerant of others. However, I still occasionally lose my patience with others, especially if they do not take my advice and keep making the same mistakes.

After much reflection, I examined my impatience under the light of Jesus Christ's words and identified the factors that were pushing my "impatient buttons." To turn the tables on my annoyance and irritability, I decided that when my patience is tested, I have the opportunity to either make a deposit in the Bank of Frustration or the Bank of Patience. Over time, I have been able to evaluate my improvement in this area with less paid into the Bank of Frustration. I pray and ask Jesus Christ to help me to gain different perspectives so that my reactions to others can be more reflective of the words in the Bible.

Self-Judging

Like others, I have also had to cope with a tendency to be judgmental of myself. If I am going to become more patient with others, I need to start with me. I always had high expectations for myself, and if I did not reach those standards, I continued working at them until I succeeded. The concept of "Failure is not an option" was ingrained in me during my formative years.

This mindset stayed with me, even when my vision declined, and so my anxiety level increased. Obviously, after losing most of my sight, I could no longer accomplish tasks in the same way I had when I was fully sighted. Once I accepted that Jesus Christ loves me even with my limitations, I became more patient with myself.

The Scripture at John 3:16 … "For God so loved the world that he gave His only begotten Son, that whoever believes in him should not perish but have everlasting life" (NKJV) … reaffirms Christ's love for me, and I can be more patient with myself, knowing his love is sufficient to overcome my flaws.

Patience With Others

Jesus Christ is essential to relationships with others because the Bible is full of specific instructions on how we should treat each other. It is crucial for believers to heed His warning in Matthew 25:40: "Whatever you did for one of the least of these brothers and sisters of mine, you did for me" (NIV).

When I delved deeper into the reasons for my impatience with others, I became aware that I was too focused on my viewpoints—I was not listening to theirs. This revelation led me to work on my listening skills and to become more accepting of differing viewpoints.

The biggest challenge for me has been waiting for desires to be granted, and that remains a work in progress. We can use the life of Job as a role model for developing patience, but the human side of me wants visible results. Some of the Bible verses that have assisted me in this area are:

- ❖ 2 Chronicles 15:7—"Be strong and do not give up, for your work will be rewarded" (NIV).
- ❖ Galatians 6:9—"And let us not grow weary while doing good, for in due season we shall reap if we do not lose heart" (NIV).
- ❖ Isaiah 40:31—"But they that wait upon the LORD shall renew their strength" (NIV).
- ❖ James 5:8—"You too, be patient and stand firm" (NIV).

Meditating on these verses reminds me that Jesus has always been there for me in the past, and he will continue to assist me if I put my trust in him.

On several occasions I have been told that "Jesus Christ is not on your time schedule, but he is always on time." These two sentiments give me comfort that my prayers will be answered when he deems it is appropriate. So I continue to strive for patience with all things, but mostly to have patience with myself.

Whenever the negative energy of impatience invades my body, I take a deep breath, embrace the feeling, and then focus on what is agitating me. These actions always help me to pause and discover the reason for my impatience. Only then can I deal with it—accepting it and adding to the Bank of Patience. And each day begins the task anew of learning to become more patient.

Prayer

Jesus Christ, help me to pause and think of you when my patience is put to the test. Help me to release my impatience into your hands and trust that your timing is perfect. Each day give me the patience I need so that my behavior reflects to others your words in the Bible. In Jesus' name, amen!

Chapter 7: A Spirit That Values Kindness

Everyone wants to experience acts of kindness, but few are willing to go the extra mile to be kind to others. Acts of kindness can be visible and invisible, and they are found in numerous ways:

- Helping a senior citizen with their shopping needs
- Providing transportation so a neighbor can attend church
- Helping a homeless person to access resources at a community center
- Giving someone your private time so they can vent

A recent act of kindness that went viral involved a teenager from Tucson, Arizona. This youth was at a shopping mall when he saw an elderly female struggling to get into her car. He dropped everything he was doing and assisted her safely into her vehicle.[7]

Thanks to the many acts of kindness performed, the world is a better place for all of us. The Greek word for *kindness* is *chréstotés*, and the translation is "gracious, useful, and of moral excellence of character or demeanor." A Greek author once said, "No act of kindness, no matter how small, is ever wasted."[8] In my opinion, showing kindness without expecting any repayment in return is the greatest virtue one could possess.

Kindness in the Bible

When I think of the word "kindness," two poignant stories, one from the Old and the other from the New Testament, come to mind. Although Bible stories have several themes, these stories illustrate one of my definitions of kindness: to give from our resources, whether they are sparse or numerous.

Both of the widows in the stories found at 1 Kings 17:10–16 (Old Testament) and Mark 12:38–42 (New Testament) demonstrated unselfish generosity. Let us put this story in the context of Bible times: widows were considered a vulnerable population because they were the poorest of the poor. There were no social welfare systems or a husband's pension to provide resources for widows. In the two stories, both widows donated from scarcity. In other words, they had very little money but still gave some of it away. Astonishingly, both gave *abundantly* from their "lack"—their shortage of funds—displaying compassion for others.

The community that I grew up in during my formative years greatly influenced my acts of kindness. I grew up in a community where most people had limited resources, yet it was a common practice for individuals to share their resources, and still is. One of my family members saw in the 1970s, a televised interview with the late Prime Minister Michael Manley of Jamaica, by the late Gil Noble, a television reporter of the *Like It Is* show. Mr. Manley described this "culture of sharing" in response to the question, "How have your citizens who are resource strapped survived during the recession?"

To provide a context to the question, at that time, Jamaica's economy was performing extremely poorly, and a large percentage of the people did not have the financial means to provide for themselves. Mr. Manley replied, "One pot," and elaborated that it was a natural behavior for neighbors to share their resources with each other, even when they are meager, and while not knowing where their next meal is coming from. Furthermore, most members of the community believe that Jesus Christ will provide for their needs. In my own opinion, these individuals' basic needs were met. Therefore, the "one-pot" philosophy has influenced my viewpoint on sharing.

Verses That Inspire Kindness

My acts of kindness are influenced by Bible teachings. Some of the Bible verses that are a blueprint for how to treat others:

- Ephesians 4:32—"Be kind and compassionate to one another" (NIV).

- Proverbs 11:17—"Those who are kind benefit themselves, but the cruel bring ruin on themselves" (NIV)

- Colossians 3:12—"Therefore, as God's chosen people, holy and dearly loved, clothe yourselves with kindness" (NIV)

The Bible states that kindness is a crucial characteristic of believers. One of the ways that I share with others is by cooking meals. I offer my services primarily to church communities, doing something that I enjoy. It is difficult at times, especially when I am cooking in new surroundings, but I have assistance from family members and others. My gifts have never been based on any kind of compensation, but instead based on Scripture.

The Bible verse that encourages me to do the best I can with a given task is Colossians 3:23: "And whatever you do, do it heartily, as to the Lord and not to men, …" (NKJV). My interpretation of this verse has been instrumental in the ways I approach tasks.

How Disabilities Can Affect Kindness

Although being kind to others is second nature to me, my low vision has affected my ability to discern when others are in need. I cannot read my physical environment, including facial cues, body language, gestures, emotions, and other factors that would normally indicate the need for kindness. Those limitations have sometimes prevented me from performing acts of kindness. But on the positive side, I do not have to see the media's coverage of acts of unkindness that is prevalent in the news.

I also associate kindness with the power of words. Since words are empowering, I try hard to speak constructively rather than destructively. I make a concerted effort to speak precisely with words that have the ability to build people up, to heal, and to bring people together.

If you are having difficulty with performing acts of kindness, you can overcome this challenge! Research suggests that you can form a new habit by performing it for twenty-one consecutive days. Therefore, seek opportunities to make kindness a habit by carrying out random acts of kindness for more than twenty-one days.

Some actions that can make kindness a pattern of behavior in our life are:

- by first being kind to ourselves
- setting a kindness goal each day
- putting others first
- being patient with others
- decluttering our personal space and donating the excess to our favorite charities
- responding to rudeness with kindness

Prayer

Jesus Christ, open my heart so that I will respond to the needs of my sisters and brothers with an open mind. I pray each day to be sensitive to others' needs more than mine. Let me be known for kindness, and through those acts, let your words in the Bible become a reality. In Jesus' name, amen!

Chapter 8: A Spirit That Values Goodness

When I think of the eighteenth-century Methodist Church movement, I think of the simple rule for Christian living: "Do all the good you can, by all the means you can."[9] This quote is often ascribed to John Wesley. This theological statement is the backdrop for a Christian's life because they want to please Jesus Christ. However, the Apostle Paul reminds us in Romans 7:18 that displaying goodness is easier said than done because of humanity's fallen nature. Many of us can identify with Paul's struggle to do good rather than evil.

Nevertheless, with focus and attention, we can overcome the inclination to do evil and instead embrace good. Before delving deeper into this topic, I want to share my working definition of goodness: "To selflessly act on behalf of others, even when we are not in the spotlight, motivated by our love for Jesus Christ." Furthermore, the Greek term for *goodness* is *agathosune*, which takes the definition a bit further by incorporating moral character as a yardstick for measuring goodness.

Goodness Casts Light on the Darkness

Let us look at goodness through the prism of the light that can be shone into the darkness of the world and the profound influence of goodness on doing the things that are pleasing to Jesus Christ. Some of the world's darkest dungeons are poverty, human trafficking, consumerism, and addiction. All these conditions resulted from human beings' perverse behaviors. Each one of these dungeons can be found in the Bible.

Poverty

There is no single root cause for global poverty; however, in the areas of policy, we all can exert some measure of control and should support policies that are designed to improve poverty. When I read Matthew 25:40, I cannot help but think about the priority that Jesus put on taking care of another person's needs before our own. If we followed that teaching, poverty could be addressed.

Human Trafficking

The darkest of darkest activity is human trafficking, where people become enslaved and cannot escape without help. Since cruelty is associated with human trafficking, Proverbs 11:17 tells us what the ramifications of cruelty are to all: "Those who are kind benefit themselves, but the cruel bring ruin on themselves" (NIV).

Consumerism

Consumerism has risen dramatically because of the constant assault by advertisements in our 24/7 universe. The danger is that material goods—or the desire for them—will become the focus of our worship rather than Jesus. I am reminded of the danger of consumerism when I meditate on

Matthew 6:33, "But seek first his kingdom and his righteousness, and all these things will be given to you as well" (NIV).

ADDICTION

Various types of addiction hold many individuals in bondage by placing immediate gratification as the highest priority. The Bible states in Exodus 20:3 that "Thou shalt have no other Gods before me" (KJV). This Scripture illuminates the vital shift in priority that those who are addicted must make.

Combat the Darkness with Volunteering

With all the darkness in the world, experiencing a point of light can be illuminating. The term "points of light" was coined and publicized by the late President George H.W. Bush in his 1989 inauguration speech,[10] saying that everyone has something to give. He subsequently created an organization, The Points of Light Foundation (https://beone.pointsoflight.org), to encourage volunteerism. Twenty years after the creation of Points of Light, President Barak Obama proclaimed continued support for this initiative and created a complementary website, https://www.nationalservice.gov/serve, so people can find volunteer opportunities more easily.

Since all of us are at risk each day for our pendulum to swing toward the darkness of the world, I have identified some personal role models to help us on this journey.

A Perfect Example of Goodness

Like others in the world, I believe that the late Mother Teresa is an exemplary illustration of a point of life emissary. Even though vivid images of Mother Teresa taking care of the poor had long been in the media, she only caught my attention in 1995, two years before her death.

I was most moved by the images, before my initial encounter with blindness, of Mother Teresa's smile while tending to the poorest of poor on the streets of Calcutta (now Kolkata), India, amid so much squalor and suffering. For me, Mother Teresa was a floodlight shining in the remarkably thick darkness of poverty. Yet her commitment to doing good could have been derailed if she had not understood and accepted Jesus Christ's purpose for her life. Once, while begging on the streets for the poor, a person she approached for assistance threw water in her face. I can imagine Mother Theresa focusing more on the needs of the poor rather than her negative encounter with the individual.

Many aspects of Mother Teresa's life reveal goodness, but I would like to focus on three of them. First, unconditional love for others guided Mother Teresa's life. I will go out on a limb here and say that Mother Teresa went to extremes in demonstrating love. Even her detractors cannot refute my sentiment. She relinquished everything that, from the perspective of human beings, makes life pleasant—wealth, material goods, power, comforts, luxuries—to serve those who were destitute. Mother Teresa's behavior toward the most vulnerable people in one of the worst slums in the world reflects the Bible's teachings. Sometimes I wonder about my ability to replicate Mother Teresa's version of love, and know I fall short.

The second feature of Mother Teresa's life has been the long-lasting effects of her goodness on marginalized people of the world. In 1950, she established the Missionaries of Charity, consisting of approximately 4500 nuns. The sisters belonging to her congregation take care of refugees, mentally ill, sick and abandoned children, and people with AIDS globally. During a mission trip, one of my family members had the good fortune of working with these nuns taking care of HIV patients, and was changed forever. The family member, who is a nurse, spoke about the high quality, compassionate care provided to a population that is most frequently abandoned and stigmatized by society.

The third striking feature of Mother Theresa was her ability to work with others for the greater good of society. She worked with the late Pope John Paul VI to establish a 74-bed shelter inside the Vatican for the homeless men and women who often sleep on the steps of Rome's churches.

Mother Teresa taught us a lot about humility. She never took credit for her work, instead, Mother Teresa gave Jesus Christ the glory. Mother Teresa was obviously aware of the uncontrollable nature of the ego because once a person starts to take credit for their efforts, Jesus leaves the center of their life. Ultimately, that person will make decisions based on feeding their ego instead of staying the course of Jesus Christ's purpose for them. In Galatians 2:19–21, the Apostle Paul expressed this sentiment as, "It is no longer I who live, but Christ who lives in me" (ESV). This definitely brings to mind Mother Teresa's lifelong journey in making Christ the center of her life.

Trying to model even one-eighth of Mother Teresa's earthly journey would be a task practically impossible for many, but the beauty of Jesus Christ is that each time we fall, he is there to pick us up. Therefore, it is worth the daily effort to be on the side of light rather than darkness. I join each of you in praying daily for his wisdom and strength to do all the good we can by any means necessary.

Prayer

Jesus Christ, may your goodness never leave us as we bind Your words and statutes around our necks and write them on the tablet of our hearts. Help us to move into a life-style marked by goodness (light) and not to stray to the world of darkness. Please provide the opportunity each day to do good and give us the strength to pass the test. Give us also the strength to think more of others and less of our-selves. In the name of Jesus Christ, we pray,

Amen!

Chapter 9: A Spirit That Values Gentleness

The Christian trait of gentleness means different things to different people, but I associate it with humility. The late C.S. Lewis captured the essence of humility and gentleness in *The Screwtape Letters*:

"By this virtue, as by all others, [Jesus Christ] wants to turn [our] attention away from self, to him and [to our] neighbors."[11]

In the Greek text, *praotés* means "gentleness, mildness, and meekness." The virtue of humility is the underlying foundation of Christian life and, unfortunately, is rarely on display in today's society. What is on display is the opposite of humility: pride—the ego on steroids.

Many individuals spend their waking hours, either talking or tweeting about their achievements, anxiously ensuring their accomplishments supersede others. A pastor once stated in a sermon that pride is the "parent of all sins," and it is dangerous because it triggers other emotions, such as jealousy, anger, hatred (because someone is doing better than you), as well as despair, sadness, and hopelessness (that you will never become equal to others). These reactions may be completely out of character for those individuals and cause mental and emotional pain and suffering in their lives. We must pursue the fruit of the Spirit, reining in our ego, and neutralizing pride with humility. That would certainly be a good beginning.

Blindness Affected My Pride

Losing my sight and becoming dependent on others made me more sensitive to the danger of my pride. During the initial stage of my blindness, I had to learn that

- my emergencies are not emergencies to others
- my mobility is somewhat dependent on others
- my ability to go to my place of worship might be out of my control
- my phobia about learning new things might very well inhibit my ability to use available technology

Overall, I had little control over many aspects of myself. As I mentioned earlier, even someone moving my toothbrush could negatively affect my normal routine.

Because the pride dwelling in me can be robust and dominant, developing humility proved to be a daunting task. One of my rationales for becoming humbler was because God commands us to do so in Proverbs 3:34 "Surely He scorns the scornful, But gives grace to the humble" (NKJV) and 1 Peter 5:5–6 " Likewise you younger people, submit yourselves to *your* elders. Yes, all of *you* be submissive to one another, and be clothed with humility, for "God resists the proud, but gives grace to the humble." Therefore, humble yourselves under the mighty hand of God, that He may exalt you in due time" (NKJV). Moreover, in Luke 1:37, the Bible says: "For with God nothing will be impossible" (NKJV). This thought comforted and reassured me. I am not alone on this unnerving journey to rid myself of pride. To address this issue and learn to become humble, I had to gain a better understanding of the detrimental effects of pride on the Christian lifestyle.

The epicenter of pride is ego, one of the three areas of the psyche. The ego is responsible for mediating between the self and the perception of reality. From my vantage point, the ego can become an albatross around one's neck because it has to be fed, attended to, and pampered. I might go to the extreme and define it as a "phantom." The ego is usually on display in high-stakes areas, such as times when the monetary gain is available. The chance of adding to a person's wealth frequently results in them becoming more preoccupied with themselves.

Whenever the ego is on display during human interactions, the goal of individuals is to become members of the preferred inner circle. Once there, the internal conversations with pride typically revolve around:

- ❖ Am I smarter?
- ❖ Am I clever?
- ❖ Can I outmatch everyone in my space?
- ❖ What do I value?

Unfortunately, the amount of energy that must be expended to jockey for power is futile. Whoever gains prominence is at risk for others to use underhanded plots and schemes to derail them. Conversely, pride can be a good thing if it motivates others to become the best versions of themselves. Nonetheless, the destructive element of pride can be seen when someone becomes "me-centric," resulting in the "ego on steroids" displaying itself in what might be thought of as low-stake environments—places of worship—causing discord among the congregants. Some individuals in places of worship have assumed specific responsibilities with the underlying motive to get noticed and acknowledged. If recognition is not forthcoming, conflict could be an outcome.

Unfortunately, those who want to step up and serve the congregation might unknowingly be doing so because of pride. They may not realize their true motive is recognition, instead of wanting to serve. And when this happens, the prideful outcome of the "ego on steroids" is that people become elevated, and Jesus Christ becomes less significant.

Erasing Pride and Magnifying Jesus Christ

How can we put to death the spirit of pride, liberate ourselves, and allow our true selves to emerge? First and foremost, we must realize that everything we have is a gift from Jesus Christ. While many individuals support the notion that their success is self-made, we are reminded in 1 Chronicles 29:14 "But who am I, and who are my people, that we should be able to give as generously as this? Everything comes from you, and we have given you only what comes from your hand" (NIV), that Jesus is the architect of our gifts.

Second, we need to turn our attention away from ourselves to Jesus Christ. This can be very hard!! Jesus deserves our attention not only because he requires us to be humble, but also because of the benefits of humility that he has explained. In Isaiah 66:1–2, God states that humility attracts his attention: "Heaven is My throne, And the earth is My footstool. Where is the house that you will build Me?

And where is the place of My rest? For all those things My hand has made, And all those things exist," says the LORD. "But on this one will I look: On him who is poor and of a contrite spirit, And who trembles at My word" (NKJV). An outstanding example of Christ's value of humility is in James 4:6–7,10: "But He gives more grace. Therefore, He says: 'God [Jesus Christ] resists the proud, but gives grace to the humble.' Therefore, submit to God [Jesus Christ]. Resist the devil, and he will flee from you … Humble yourselves in the sight of the Lord, and He will lift you up" (NKJV).

Another vital action in liberating myself from pride has been continuous self-evaluation of my actions and honest admission of my flaws. Since pride is subtle, sneaky, and shows up in unexpected places, one has always to evaluate the motives for responses to situations. A question that could be a guide during this period would be: Is my answer pleasing to Man or Jesus Christ?

Who Are You Pleasing?

Trying to please human beings is futile because of their innate unpredictable nature. Becoming a "people-pleaser" can lead to over-performance and then to burnout. A person who is always worried about what other people think will also increase their risk for rejection and emotional turmoil. The worst result is that Jesus will move to the periphery of their life.

On the other hand, pleasing Jesus Christ by following his pattern of behavior, will strengthen our spirit of humility. Some examples of Jesus' humility are listed below, and following them will help keep one's pride in check.

- He accepted being in lowly places, not only entering lavish residences but also simple homes.

- He helped people who had nothing to repay him with.

- He showed a grateful heart, thanking God out loud in his public prayers.

- He was willing to forgive others for their sins, both against him and against others.

- He avoided the accolades people wanted to award him with.

The spiritual and emotional benefits of developing humility outweigh any physical prosperity a person might gain with inflated pride. Although it is hard to be humble, especially in our 24/7 technological world, we must do the best we can to acquire this spiritual characteristic if our ultimate goal is to please Jesus Christ. As I continue to walk with Jesus, it becomes more critical for me to develop the spirit of humility.

Prayer

O Lord, instruct me to be meek and humble. Let my ears and heart be closed to the praise that comes from man and not to yearn to sit in the seat of recognition. Grant, O Lord, that I may look for nothing, claim nothing, and that I may go through all the scenes of life not seeking my glory, but looking wholly unto you. Help me not to follow the lure of the false promises of pride. In the name of Jesus Christ, we pray, amen!

Chapter 10: A Spirit That Values Faithfulness

Faith and faithfulness are inextricably linked. Faith, the basic foundation of the Judeo-Christian doctrine, means having complete trust and confidence in a higher power. Faithfulness, on the other hand, is having long-term continued and steadfast fidelity to something. The underpinning of faithfulness is faith, and therefore, the focus of this discussion will be on faith.

The Greek word for *faith* and *faithful* is *pistis*, translated as "belief, firm persuasion, assurance, and firm conviction." Most people have an innate sense that there is something greater than self. The drive to discover what that might be has continued for millennia. Many searchers have not figured out that discovering something more significant than self happens during the Christian journey.

What is faith? In my opinion, faith is "entrusting oneself to God." We are reminded in Hebrews 11:1 "Now faith is the substance of things hoped for, the evidence of things not seen" (NKJV), that faith is trusting in Jesus Christ, being unshakably confident that what we hope for will be received according to his time. A visual image of faith is in Luke 5:12–16. While Jesus was in one of the towns, a man who was covered with leprosy but with unwavering faith in Jesus Christ's healing power came along. When he saw Jesus, he fell with his face to the ground and begged him, "Lord, if you are willing, you can make me clean." Jesus reached out his hand and touched the man, saying "I am willing; be cleansed." Immediately the leprosy left him.

Nonetheless, a lot of people experience what could be called "faith inertia," and this comes about due to many reasons. An issue that might affect one's faith might be a crisis that cannot be reconciled with one's beliefs, such as 9/11, ethnic cleansing, etc. Increasing our faith begins with spending dedicated time with Jesus Christ's words. In the Bible, a comprehensive definition of faith, with examples, is found in Hebrews 11:1–39, especially verse 6: "...without faith it is impossible to please God" (NKJV).

The Benefits of Faith

The Bible promises that when a faithful person pleases Jesus by expressing their faith, some of the benefits we can receive are gaining the desires of our heart, eternal life, provision for our needs, and allowing us to live at peace with our enemies. Furthermore, faith increases by listening to the words of Jesus Christ. Romans 10:17 "So then faith *comes* by hearing, and hearing by the word of God" (NKJV) encourages one to feed oneself with Jesus Christ's words because it will change a person's perspectives, helping them to view things from His viewpoint.

Faith also grows through believing and trusting Jesus' words. If we believe and trust him, we can be the beneficiary of the following promises:

- "I [Jesus Christ] will never leave you nor forsake you." Hebrews 13:5 (NKJV)
- Joy and peace for those who trust him. Romans 15:13

- A sense of well-being in regard to overcoming obstacles. Psalm 112:7

- Protection against those who will try to inflict harm. Isaiah 54:17

I am no different than other people because, at times, I too struggle with my faith. Sometimes I am guilty of thinking that my faith is strong enough to withstand life's ups and downs, and when I meet life's sword on the road, I typically try to take things into my own hands rather than wait on Jesus to fix the problem. But I have found that whenever I try to take care of these challenges of life, my stress level increases, and my focus shifts toward the potential doom and gloom of the circumstances.

As my desire to increase my faith became more prominent, I acted on Jesus Christ's words by taking a leap of faith in one of my goals and, for example, applying for a job when I had no idea how I was going to get to work every day.

Walking and Cooking By Faith

After I was declared legally blind, I took a leap of faith by accepting a job in a kitchen, which was an unlikely environment for someone who is blind. I was responsible for prepping the food that was to be cooked and occasionally cooking. My day began at four o'clock in the morning with prayers, and I arrived at work by five a.m. Starting my day with prayer reassured me that Jesus Christ would be there to guide and protect me at work.

My daily activities consisted of using potentially dangerous equipment to shred or slice onions, celery, and vegetables. Slicing equipment accidents can happen easily to sighted people who are not paying attention, so I had to pay more than the usual attention to avoid being injured! Moreover, I had to cut and prepare various meats for cooking. While preparing food, I also had to be vigilant about my safety.

I began each day with the goal of providing the highest quality food to the consumers, and I was able to be successful in that area under challenging circumstances because of my strong beliefs in Jesus Christ's provisions. I hope that I am not giving the impression that this journey was easy because it was not. It was very difficult, but I was able to overcome the obstacles because I tried to focus on the positive experiences of the environment rather than the negative.

I also had to deal with some negative attitudes from my peers, and there were actually some coworkers who tried to derail my efforts. Whenever I suggested to them that we should work together to produce a better product, they ridiculed me with the following slogan: "Play the hero and you'll get zero."

To compound the situation, the turnover rate for employees was very high, and the employer did not put any effort into reversing this trend. Working in an ever-changing and hostile environment while trying to put out the best quality products and accomplishing that goal could only happen through having faith in Jesus Christ.

Faith Conquers Fear

One of my biggest fears has been walking alone on the street. Although I was aware of the services available from the Lighthouse organization for the blind, I never took advantage of them because I feared change. Since each city/state Lighthouse organization has its own unique URL, I have provided the links for three states:

- Fort Worth, Texas: https://lighthousefw.org/client-services/

- San Francisco, California: http://lighthouse-sf.org/

- Tampa, Florida: https://tampalighthouse.org/

Nonetheless, I prayed that Jesus would take away my concerns and give me the strength to take and utilize the services. Over time my anxiety dissipated, and I sought the assistance of the Lighthouse and worked with a mobile instructor to learn to cross streets safely, even those with several lanes. While working with the mobile instructor, I would quietly repeat Joshua 1:9 to myself: "Be strong and of good courage; do not be afraid, nor be dismayed, for the LORD your God *is* with you wherever you go" (NKJV)

Repeating this verse helped me to shift my focus away from my fears onto the activities at hand. Fast forward—I can now use a "white cane" to independently cross streets with multiple lanes.

Strengthening My Faith

Based on my pastor's teachings, there are three ways that I can strengthen my faith.

First, I confidently go to Jesus Christ about my needs. One of my prayers is asking for an increase in my faith. Matthew 6:8 reads, "Therefore, do not be like them. For your Father knows the things you have need of before you ask Him." (NKJV)

Second, I persist in prayer. In the Parable of the Persistent Widow in Luke 18:1–8, Jesus taught his disciples the importance of praying unceasingly.

And third, I ask Jesus Christ to forgive my transgressions. A lack of repentance will create a wall between myself and him, so I want to make sure that none exists.

My stress level has reduced because of my growth in faith. Most importantly, whenever I need assistance, more often than not, there is someone to assist me. I call these individuals "angels of mercy." Many of them have left me in awe because they were so generous with their time. Having unwavering faith is an absolute necessity for the Christian life, and it is a walk I gladly take each day.

Prayer

Heavenly Father, I thank you that you are true to your promises. Help me to trust you entirely with my life. Help me to have faith in you even when I do not see what I expect to see. Jesus Christ, I choose to believe you. I prefer to trust you because I have faith in your words. In the name of Jesus Christ, we pray, amen!

Chapter 11: A Spirit That Values Forgiveness

During the last two decades, the United States has experienced multiple national tragedies—events of a kind that had never happened before. They affected us in different ways. Some people felt a sense of loss or helplessness, while others looked for answers as to why these things happened. Some of the tragedies that have pulled on my heartstrings are the 9/11 attacks in New York City, a 2006 Amish school shooting in Pennsylvania, the 2015 church shooting in Charleston, South Carolina; and the 2018 Tree of Life congregation shooting in Pittsburgh, Pennsylvania. Family members of the deceased individuals' lives had been changed. The Greek word for *forgiveness* is *aphiemi*, translated as to remit or forgive sins.

When I ponder the Bible's interpretation of forgiveness, I think of the many families who were affected by the Amish school and Charleston church shootings because, in both cases, the families forgave the perpetrator. Their forgiveness did not waver even though the South Carolina perpetrator stated after the hideous act that he has not shed a tear for his action—or his victims—because he has no regrets.

How have these families been able to cope with their senseless loss and to muster the strength to exercise the virtue of forgiveness? I do not know the answer to the question. However, I believe these exceptional individuals are role models for us all.

Biblical Forgiveness

Merriam-Webster Collegiate Dictionary defines forgiveness as "to cease to feel resentment against perceived offenders; to give up resentment of others and forgive them for their transgressions." Many individuals in the world support this definition, but I will go further in saying that there are two types of forgiveness: human and biblical.

On the human side, some people believe that they have let go of resentment, but behind closed doors, they keep revisiting the incident, hoping that through serendipity or fate, the score will be settled in the future. Conversely, biblical forgiveness is living out our faith through letting go of resentment immediately and completely and empathizing with the offender because we are all imperfect beings.

The noticeable component of biblical forgiveness is having unconditional love for the offender. Note that forgiveness does not mean that we should allow the offender to continue to abuse us or that we are to pretend that the incident never occurred. Nevertheless, not forgiving a person—also known as "holding a grudge"—will interfere with our relationship with Jesus Christ. Our mind and heart will be filled with negative thoughts rather than the inspiring words of the Bible.

The virtue of forgiveness is a big one for me because it is a process, and it takes commitment and time. I do not believe that I am at the place of those aforementioned families. But I continue to push myself to get to the place of forgiving readily and consequently letting go of any feelings of victimization.

When I am hard on myself or others, I contemplate the following questions:

- ❖ Am I being too sensitive?
- ❖ Do I set the bar too high for others?

Regarding sensitivity and my expectations of others, I reflect on these questions:

- ❖ Do I take things personally?
- ❖ Do I reflect more on the negative aspects of interactions rather than positive?
- ❖ Do I have unrealistic expectations of others?
- ❖ Am I self-critical?
- ❖ Am I fearful of the word "no"?
- ❖ Do I take ownership of other people's behavior?
- ❖ Is my behavior affected by the actions of others?

Gauging Sensitivity

In the areas that keep challenging me, I have sought assistance from others. If I am not able to overcome my sensitivity, I will always be in a vulnerable position emotionally and even spiritually.

If I notice I have become overly critical or judgmental of myself or others, I contemplate the following questions:

- ❖ Am I a perfectionist?

- ❖ Do I beat myself up over a mistake?
- ❖ Do I have difficulty praising others?
- ❖ Do I have an opinion on everything?

One of the ways to deal with this area is to find the positive in everything. Moreover, the Bible plays a pivotal role in assisting me in developing the virtue of forgiveness. In Matthew 18:21–22, "Then Peter came to Him and said, "Lord, how often shall my brother sin against me, and I forgive him? Up to seven times?" (NKJV). Jesus instructs his disciples that they must forgive without limitations. We are reminded of the importance of forgiving others so we can be assured of Jesus Christ's forgiveness for us. Furthermore, Matthew 18:21–35, the Parable of the Unforgiving Servant, provides a striking example of the ramifications of not following the Bible's instructions. A servant whose enormous debt was forgiven by his master did not offer the same forgiveness to his debtor, a man who owed the servant a miniscule amount in proportion to what he had owed the master (NKJV). Jesus concludes this story with a less-than-comforting proclamation in Matthew 18:35: "So My Heavenly Father also will do to you if each of you, from his heart, does not forgive his brother his trespasses" (NKJV). One of the most renowned texts on forgiveness is in the Lord's Prayer, found in Matthew 6:9–13. In particular, in verse 12, we hear Jesus' instruction: "And forgive us our debts, As we forgive our debtors" (NKJV).

While I was working on forgiveness, one day, I got a front-seat view of my progress. It was a typical workday, and I arrived at the site and started preparing food for lunch. On this particular day, I was running a bit late with cooking the food. Unbeknown to me, one of my coworkers, Mark, with whom I had an adversarial relationship, came into my work area and left a cup of coffee on the table. Of course, I was not aware that I had accidentally overturned his coffee. While I was carrying a large pot of hot cooked meat from the stove to the warmer, Mark threw the residue of the coffee in my face. I was caught off guard and did not know what had provoked his action.

Shortly afterward, the restaurant owner called me in to discuss Mark's complaint, which was that I "violated him by overturning his coffee." To make matters worse, in my opinion, it appeared that the owner was more sympathetic to Mark's interpretation of the incident than mine. I was stunned and became lost for words at the time, which interfered with my ability to continue working. When I got my bearings back, I recited the Lord's Prayer to myself because I find the words comforting. The more I quietly repeated this prayer, the more I relaxed and was able to think of the next step. Before the end of the workday, I apologized to Mark and offered reimbursement for the coffee, which he declined. In retrospect, I was able to apologize before the day ended because my priority had shifted away from me and to Mark. I only have control over my actions, not the other person's. I want Jesus Christ's words to live through me rather than bitterness and resentment.

Prayer

Jesus, thank you for forgiving me, no matter how many times I fall. I want to be a forgiving person. Reveal to me those who I have overlooked. Help me to see the positive side of interactions and to let go of the thoughts that are not of you. In the name of Jesus Christ, we pray, amen!

Chapter 12: A Spirit That Values Wisdom

Family conflicts and divorce rates continue to escalate in the modern world, causing the disintegration of the family unit. This kind of turbulence can have lasting effects for generations. In the workplace, the majority of employees deal with conflict on some level, and that adds up to billions of dollars lost for paid time off. Geopolitical conflicts have been escalating over the years, using up trillions of dollars that could have been used to enhance the quality of life for individuals with the least resources.

We just cannot get along!! Why not?

The Greek word for wisdom is *sophia*, meaning the ability to judge correctly and to follow the best course of action. Oftentimes, our course of action in the church leads to conflict. Since church communities are microcosms of society, it is not surprising that an anonymous Twitter survey indicated that conflicts in churches are rising. Frequently, the causes are absurd. Like "Believer A was singing too loud and off-key, and it made it impossible for me to sing properly." Or "Believer B always comes in late, breaking my concentration and disrespecting the congregation."

Many pastors have associated these conflicts with a lack of wisdom. Wisdom, as defined by Merriam-Webster, means "ability to discern inner qualities and relationships; good sense"—in other words, having knowledge, good judgment, and the ability to see the long-term (or bigger) picture.

Church communities have been pivotal in sharing Christian values with the rest of the world. Services provide opportunities for believers to learn about the gospel, ask questions to clarify misconceptions, work together on different initiatives, support each other during difficult times, and pray together. Furthermore, stable congregations are fundamental for expansion. Dedicated spaces allow individuals to connect with a higher power.

For me, the church community gives me a sense of purpose. One reason is that I am aware that conflicts are almost inevitable between congregation members, and that provides me with an occasion to help reduce tensions. Teaching people how to exercise wisdom will lead to a reduction in church conflicts. Also, it is an essential virtue for Christians if they want to foster unity.

King Solomon's Wisdom

In the biblical world, King Solomon's name is synonymous with wisdom. Solomon was one of King David's sons and was credited with building the first temple in Jerusalem. He also wrote three inspired books in the Bible: Ecclesiastes, the Song of Solomon (also known as "Canticles" or Song of Songs), and most of Proverbs. During Solomon's early reign as king, God told him that he could have whatever he desired because of his obedience. Solomon could have had anything, but he chose wisdom.

The story at 1 Kings 3:16–28 is an example of Solomon's wisdom and great insight. Two women claimed to be the mother of a child, and Solomon had to decide who was the biological mother. The benefits of DNA testing were unavailable at that time, so Solomon's decision had to be based on what he knew of the world and what he knew of the Bible. He ordered the child to be split into two and observed the reactions of both women. Then he ruled in favor of the woman who did not want the child to be divided, and his fame spread wide and far.

The Wisdom in the Book of Proverbs

Previously I was familiar with the word "wisdom," but had only applied it to intellectual ability, not to one's actions. Because the stable cohesiveness of my church community has become necessary to me, I want to gain wisdom so I can navigate and improve challenging relationships in my congregation. I sought my pastor's advice on ways to develop understanding and was encouraged to read the Book of Proverbs and apply it to my life's situations. Although this assignment continues to be a work in process, I have learned a lot from Proverbs and want to share some snippets of the book that have been most beneficial.

One theologian, Dr. Henrietta C. Mears,[12] divided the Book of Proverbs the following ways:

- Chapter 1–10: Advice for Young People
- Chapters 11–20: Advice for All People
- Chapters 21–31: Advice for Rulers

I have approached the gospel based on this outline and found that this Bible book has been invaluable in providing advice for different areas of my life. Furthermore, Proverbs consists of 31 chapters. If a person reads one chapter each day, especially in the months with 31 days, they will have read it all. However, I have been focusing more on the first 20 chapters because the last 11 chapters apply to leaders.

Let us discuss the verses that provide insight into building relationships. The second verse of the first chapter laid the groundwork for my study.

Proverbs 1:2: "To know wisdom and instruction; to perceive the words of understanding,…" (NKJV).

I appreciate the information detailed in Proverbs that a clear understanding of the difference between knowledge and wisdom is beneficial. In this fast-paced technological world, it is crucial to apply information progressively to derive solutions. However, wisdom allows one to become more perceptive during the decision-making process, a skill necessary to function in a world where human beings are unpredictable, and environments are fluid.

Many times conflict could be quickly resolved, but pride hinders resolution. Proverbs 13:10, "By pride comes nothing but strife, But with the well-advised *is* wisdom" (NKJV), warns us of the detrimental effects of pride on relationships. As I mentioned earlier, one of the causes of conflict within a church is the rumor mill. To combat that tendency, Proverbs 18:21, "The tongue has the power of life and death, and those who love it will eat its fruit" (NIV), talk about the importance of listening rather than speaking, especially when disparaging things are being said about others—either by yourself or someone else.

Proverbs 13:5 "A righteous man hateth lying: but a wicked man is loathsome, and cometh to shame" (KJV), reinforces the importance of honesty and integrity in relationships with others and the irreparable damage that can occur to one's reputation when he is slandered by others. Once an individual's reputation is destroyed, it is tough to restore it.

In addition, Proverbs 15:1 "A soft answer turneth away wrath: but grievous words stir up anger" (KJV) offers crucial advice on ways to avoid unhealthy conflicts. Proverbs 11:2 "When pride cometh, then cometh shame: but with the lowly is wisdom" (KJV) identifies the link between wisdom and humility, a quality that can help promote positive, long-lasting relationships.

Wisdom in the Church Community

Believers have to continually work hard on building stronger relationships with each other. Some of the simple principles I have found success with to improve ties with my spiritual family are:

- To be patient with each other
- Counteract negative statements with positive ones
- Understand that people are petty
- Avoid becoming entangled in any pettiness
- Remain focused on the church's goal
- Diffuse gossiping
- Promote healing

Gaining wisdom should continue to be every believer's goal. Wisdom is a part of that cluster of attitudes in our personalities, enhancing worshiping communities. Believers should keep striving for knowledge and insight regarding biblical qualities, and wisdom will abound. Most notably, the more wisdom that is applied by Christians in their worshiping communities, the more frequently incredible things can happen.

Prayer

Almighty Jesus Christ, I pray that you will give me wisdom and understanding in all things. Increase wisdom in me so that I can see the truth in all things. Make me be a wise person who moves by your teachings. May I always seek your counsel in every situation. In the name of Jesus Christ, we pray, amen!

Chapter 13: A Spirit That Values Gratitude

Each morning when I wake up, I have two choices: to complain about what I am lacking or to be grateful for my countless blessings. I have sat and listened to many church sermons on the benefits of having an attitude of gratefulness. One pastor, whose name I cannot recall, says that gratitude is the most significant spiritual practice there is, and he emphasized the fantastic benefits on the body:

- decreased stress levels
- decreased anxiety levels
- gratitude fosters humility, which lessens the chances of our being injured by pride
- gratitude makes us less critical of others, which improves our relationship with others
- gratitude makes us more positive and happier, which lessens the chances of disease because the body's hormonal levels tend to be balanced rather than fluctuate

During that particular sermon, the pastor implored his listeners to be thankful even during difficult times and that doing so would be an indication of spiritual growth. Displaying gratitude, even during tumultuous times, is such anti-human nature that is easier said than done. Marcus Tullius Cicero, a Roman philosopher, said, "A thankful heart is not only the greatest virtue, but the parent of all other virtues."[13] Gratitude enhances other virtues, encouraging us to reflect more on what the Bible teaches. The Greek word for gratitude is *eucharistia*, meaning thankfulness.

My family has a long-standing tradition on Thanksgiving. Before proceeding with the meal, family members and friends list what they are thankful for. Similarly, in my prayer group, we have dedicated a segment to thanking Jesus Christ for his blessings. Expressing gratitude should not be confined to specific events but should be a daily, ongoing activity. Here are some of the attitudes and actions that I practice to increase my spirit of gratitude.

Cultivate Gratitude With Others

One of the first ways I cultivate an attitude of gratefulness is by doing my best to be involved with a circle of friends who themselves are grateful people. If I find myself needing to interact with individuals who do not possess this trait, I firmly but lovingly try to reframe any conversation that is going down the road of ungratefulness.

A lack of appreciation for the blessings in our life can be so ingrained in people that they do not even recognize it. So it's important for all of us to be around people who are grateful because the behavior is contagious. Life has its struggles, but isn't it refreshing to spend time with people who are thankful for the smallest rose in their life? We can almost feel our spirits lifting when we're around someone who is willing to see the blessings in their circumstances.

TAKE TIME TO CULTIVATE GRATITUDE

Another approach is to take the time to be filled with gratitude. I have dedicated the end of the day, before I go to bed, to focus on my daily blessings. This exercise has put me in touch with my expectations and helps me to control any negative feelings or thoughts that arise. Most importantly, this practice consciously conditions my mind to see roses rather than withered flowers.

When I am deliberately cultivating this mindset, I see that I become more appreciative of things that frequently get overlooked, such as nature, sun, snow, caregivers, etc. Like anyone else, I find that practicing gratitude under challenging times is a work in progress. However, during those times, I focus more on what is right about the situation and try to be grateful for those things. I also consider lessons that I can learn from the circumstances and pray to Jesus Christ for insight during future interactions.

In addition, I repeat the following prayer—or a similar version of it—before going to bed:

Dear Jesus Christ:

Thank you ever so much for today and for being with me throughout the day, especially during challenging times. Thank you for my blessings and helping me to move around my surroundings independently and safely. Thank you for the good and bad experiences, and help me to learn from my negative encounters. Thank you for the people you put in my life to assist me on this journey.

Please increase my confidence in you so that I do not lose hope when my life appears to fall apart. Free my mind of life's distractions so that I can have a restful night.

Thank you, thank you, thank you, for everything.

In the name of Jesus Christ, we pray. Amen!

In Jesus' name, amen!

Giving to Others Cultivates Gratitude

Another activity that helps me to develop the spirit of gratitude is ministering to others. Jesus reminds us in Luke 10:27b to "Love your neighbor as yourself" (NIV). What better way to love our neighbor than by serving them? My self-centeredness becomes less when I serve my neighbor, and I also become more appreciative of my abundant blessings.

If we want to boost our virtue of gratitude, consider participating in a mission trip to minister to the poor outside of the US. I have done it, and my appreciation for blessings always goes up to 1000 percent.

Developing Gratitude Every Day

The Bible encourages its readers to develop a spirit of gratitude, and if we want to develop this trait, we must commit ourselves to memorize selected gems from Jesus Christ's words. Becoming familiar with verses of gratitude from the Bible will enable us to share them with others, adding real substance to our conversations.

In the Old Testament, appreciation is one of the main elements of worship in many chapters of the Book of Psalms. One of the most commonly read chapters is Psalm 23. Verse 1 says, "The Lord is my Shepherd; I shall not want" (KJV). Meditating on it will put us at ease regarding our daily needs. Jesus promises that what we need will be taken care of, so we should be grateful for his kindness. If we can rest on that promise, our reduced daily stress level will affect our health positively.

GRATITUDE TO JESUS CHRIST

One of the ways that believers display their relationship with Jesus Christ is through worship, which is also important to him. But there are times when we are busy with our daily activities and forget to show our gratefulness by praising him. Psalm 86:12 says, "I will praise You, O Lord my God, with all my heart, …" (NKJV). It is an excellent verse to commit to memory to remind us of this necessity.

Another of the Apostle Paul's instructions on the general role of Christian behavior is in Colossians 3:23: "Whatever you do, work at it with all your heart, as working for the Lord, not for human masters, …" (NIV).

In summation, our decisions and actions should encourage, facilitate, and display thanksgiving to Jesus Christ.

Assisting Others

There are two vulnerable populations for whom I have a strong affinity: children and the elderly. Regarding children, my wife and I ensure that the children who cross our path are treated kindly.

We visit local nursing homes for the elderly and tend to some of the needs of the people living there. Some of the residents have outlived their children or are from fractured families. We sing with them, and for those who want to talk about the Bible, we have lively discussions. I have learned that the Bible has many interpretations and can be controversial, but on the other hand, I have learned more about the Bible and world events from these talks. Many of these residents have experienced several wars during the twentieth century and the Depression-era and are therefore well qualified to offer pearls of wisdom. We are grateful that they give us the opportunity to be with them and learn from them.

Finally, let us not only express gratitude during a special season or event. Instead, let daily gratitude shape our heart, mind, attitude, and actions. We are in a win-win situation if we adopt a spirit of appreciation because our body will be healthier rather than being unhealthy. Make a daily effort to practice the virtue of gratitude.

Prayer

Almighty Jesus Christ, thank you for giving me the opportunity to see another day. I can get out of bed, and many people are unable to do so. Please provide for their needs. Please guide my actions today so that my thinking and behavior reflect a spirit of thanksgiving. Could you help me to see each day as a gift? I pray that you will increase the spirit of appreciation in my foes and friends and those in my biological, marital, and spiritual families.

In the name of Jesus Christ, we pray, amen!

Chapter 14: Checking in on Me!!!

Over the last five years, I have been participating in what I call a "spiritual workout." My sessions in the presence of Jesus Christ have become longer and are now more focused on building a good relationship with him. At times I sought out Jesus for a miracle, only wanting a physical need or desire fulfilled. Sometimes it was easy for me to fall into this childlike relationship with him, praying for this or that because I assumed if the favor was granted, I would become happy or be more fulfilled. It still happens occasionally, and it is at those times, when my focus is lost, that it becomes important for me to remember that Jesus Christ is my Lord and Savior—not a magical person who fulfills my wish list.

During these workouts, I have also learned how challenging the Christian walk can be in a modern world with so many distractions and shifting values. Since I cannot control the changes in society, I choose to keep my eyes on the prize: Jesus Christ. Our Omnipotent Christ tells us in the inspired words of the Bible to keep asking, seeking, and knocking at his door, and most crucially, to pray unceasingly. He knows how easy it is for humankind to take back the crosses placed at his feet and try to resolve them on our own.

I am an active member of a church community and continue to work on building my characteristics of love, joy, peace, patience, kindness, goodness, faithfulness, gentleness, and self-control, along with forgiveness, wisdom, and gratitude. Furthermore, I am full of hope that Jesus Christ plans to use me in mighty ways.

I have had the aim of owning a restaurant, and the name for it that comes to my thought is ELIJAYH (a combination of my two grandsons' names). Although this is my desire, Jesus Christ has the final say, and I am patiently waiting for him to make it a reality or not. My approach to waiting on his intercession for the restaurant has been influenced by Psalm 37:23 "The steps of a good man are ordered by the Lord" (NKJV).

My spiritual workout has transformed me into a person who is more patient, accepting of others' imperfections, prayerful, and nonjudgmental; full of gratitude for the smallest thing, helping individuals to close the gap between differences, putting people ahead of material things, and being sensitive to others' needs and advocating for them if necessary; being a peacemaker who is forgiving, kind, and loves others; being empathetic, compassionate, and humble; and most importantly, a person who loves to worship Jesus Christ.

ART
IS MY
FAVORITE
SPORT

About The Author

Marcia Theresa Caton is a mother, nurse, educator, coach, and motivational speaker, who has led workshops and seminars on various topics locally and globally for the past two decades. Because Marcia juggles many roles, she knows how surprising, unpredictable, and stressful everyday life can be in our 24/7 world. Furthermore, Marcia knows how easy it is to become discouraged when life throws a curveball. Therefore, she felt the urgency to share Clive Clarke's story, who had experienced a significant life change in a short period and is determined to remain positive. Since experiencing life adversity is a common denominator for everyone, Marcia hopes that Clive's life journey will become an exemplar for those with challenges not to: embrace victimization identity, have a pity party, or ask "why me." Rather than feeling down-trodden by adversities, individuals should look at these challenges through the virtue of gratitude. This mindset will allow you to develop a positive frame of mind and reboots your spirit to fight rather than flight.

References

Strong's Exhaustive Concordance of the Bible. Accessed April 17, 2019. https://biblehub.com/strongs.htm.

Merriam Webster's Collegiate Dictionary. 2014. Springfield: Merriam-Webster.

Endnotes

[1] The term *spirit* has several connotations, so for this book I define it as "having the attitude, disposition, and passion that would be pleasing to Jesus Christ."

[2] "Pierre Teilhard De Chardin Quotes (Author of The Phenomenon of Man)." n.d. Goodreads. Goodreads. Accessed September 4, 2018. https://www.goodreads.com/author/quotes/5387.Pierre_Teilhard_de_Chardin.

[3] Einstein, Albert, Alice Calaprice, and Albert Einstein. 2005. *The New Quotable Einstein*. Princeton, NJ: Princeton University Press.

[4] "Let There Be Peace on Earth (Song)." 2018. Wikipedia. Wikimedia Foundation. May 15, 2018. https://en.wikipedia.org/wiki/Let_There_Be_Peace_on_Earth_(song).

[5] Stress symptoms: Effects on your body and behavior, Mayo Clinic. Accessed May 25, 2019.

[6] Arnold, Johann Christoph. n.d. "Steven McDonald's Story." Plough. Accessed December 24, 2018. https://www.plough.com/en/topics/life/forgiveness/steven-mcdonalds-story.

[7] Janssen, Heather. 2018. "Tucson Teen Goes Viral for Helping Old Woman Walk to Her Car." Https://Www.kold.com. August 11, 2018. https://www.kold.com/story/38861811/tucson-teen-goes-viral-for-helping-old-woman-walk-to-her-car/.

[8] "Aesop." n.d. Wikiquote. Accessed April 17, 2019. https://en.wikiquote.org/wiki/Aesop.

[9] Wesley, J. John Wesley Quote. Retrieved on January 24, 2019 from https://www.passiton.com/inspirational-quotes/7155-do-all-the-good-you-can-by-all-the-means-you.

[10] Whitaker, Morgan. 2017. "Here's What George H.W. Bush Said in His Inauguration Speech." AOL.com. AOL. February 23, 2017. https://www.aol.com/article/news/2017/01/19/president-george-h-w-bushs-first-inauguration-speech-full-te/21658319/.

[11] Lewis, C S. 1982. *The Screwtape Letters*. New York, NY: Harper Collins.

[12] Mears, H.C. (2011). *What the Bible Is All About*. Regal Books, Ventura: California

[13] "A Thankful Heart Is Not Only the Greatest Virtue, but the Parent of All Other Virtues." n.d. Marcus Tullius Cicero: A Thankful Heart Is Not Only the Greatest Virtue, but the Parent of All Other Virtues. Accessed January 26, 2019. https://www.quotes.net/quote/7027.

Made in the USA
Columbia, SC
05 May 2021